WAYNE GRETZKY

HOCKEY LEGEND

BY LUKE HANLON

Book design by Jake Nordby
Cover design by Jake Nordby

Photographs ©: AP Images, cover, 1; Bruce Bennett/Getty Images, 4–5, 8, 11, 14, 17, 20–21, 22, 25, 26; Andrew D. Bernstein/Getty Images Sport/Getty Images, 7; Robert Shaver/Bruce Bennett/Getty Images, 13; Mike Ridewood/Canadian Press/AP Images, 18, 30; Red Line Editorial, 29

Press Box Books, an imprint of Press Room Editions.

ISBN
978-1-63494-787-9 (library bound)
978-1-63494-807-4 (paperback)
978-1-63494-846-3 (epub)
978-1-63494-827-2 (hosted ebook)

Library of Congress Control Number: 2023908986

Distributed by North Star Editions, Inc.
2297 Waters Drive
Mendota Heights, MN 55120
www.northstareditions.com

Printed in the United States of America
012024

About the Author
Luke Hanlon is a sportswriter and editor based in Minneapolis.

TABLE OF CONTENTS

1 50 IN 39

Wayne Gretzky gained control of the puck just past the blue line. The 20-year-old superstar had already scored a hat trick against the Philadelphia Flyers. Now the Edmonton Oilers center was on the hunt for more goals.

As Gretzky advanced the puck, a Flyers defender charged toward him. Gretzky shifted the puck back to avoid the defender. Then he lifted his stick and rifled a slap shot into the top of the net. Three days earlier, Gretzky had scored four

Wayne Gretzky scored a career-high 92 goals during the 1981–82 season.

goals against the Los Angeles Kings. Now, on December 30, 1981, he had already scored four more against the Flyers with 15 minutes still to play. That gave Gretzky 49 goals in his 39th game of the season. No player had ever scored 50 goals in fewer than 50 games. Gretzky had a chance to reach that mark in just 39.

In the final minute of the game, the Flyers pulled their goalie to try to score a tying goal. However, Oilers forward Glenn Anderson picked up a loose puck in his defensive zone. He quickly passed it ahead to Gretzky. With the seconds winding down, Gretzky glided past a defender. That move created enough space for him to shoot from the blue line. The puck flew into the net with three seconds left.

A teammate rushed to Gretzky and hugged him down to the ice. Soon all of Gretzky's

Gretzky (right) celebrates with a teammate after the Oilers scored in a 1981 game.

teammates did, too. The fans in Edmonton rose to their feet to cheer Gretzky's achievement. It was one of many National Hockey League (NHL) records Gretzky would break.

2 HOCKEY PRODIGY

Wayne Gretzky was born on January 26, 1961, in Brantford, Ontario. He started skating when he was two. By the time he was six, Wayne was playing in a league against 11-year-olds. Despite playing against kids who were older than him, Wayne dominated. In his final season of peewee hockey, he scored 378 goals.

Gretzky began his professional career in the World Hockey Association (WHA). As a 17-year-old in 1978, he signed a contract with the Indianapolis Racers.

A young Wayne Gretzky poses for a photo while playing peewee hockey.

TUCKED JERSEY

When Wayne Gretzky was playing with older kids, he had to wear a jersey that was meant for someone five years older than him. To make up for the massive jersey, he tucked it into his pants. Gretzky became so used to it that he tucked in the right side of his jersey throughout his playing career.

However, Gretzky played only eight games with the team. The Racers ended up selling his contract to the Edmonton Oilers. This sale worked out great for Edmonton. Gretzky played 72 games in his first season with the Oilers, tallying 104 points. He was so good in the WHA that the Oilers signed him to a 21-year contract on his 18th birthday in 1979.

Before the 1979–80 season, the WHA folded. Four teams from the WHA joined the NHL. The Oilers were one of those four teams.

Gretzky tucks in his jersey during a WHA game in 1979.

Gretzky now had a chance to prove himself in hockey's best league. Critics thought Gretzky would be too small to succeed in the NHL. But the 6-foot (183 cm), 185-pound (84 kg) center was used to playing against people who were bigger than him.

Just like he had at every level before that, Gretzky thrived in the NHL. He used his elite vision to provide scoring chances for teammates. The area behind the net became known as "Gretzky's office." He would set up there and feed passes to teammates. That helped him rack up huge assist numbers. In 1979–80, Gretzky led the NHL with 86 assists and 137 points. Those numbers were good enough for him to win the Hart Trophy. That award is given to the league's Most Valuable Player (MVP).

Gretzky recorded 100 or more assists in a season 11 different times.

3 THE GREAT ONE

When Wayne Gretzky was 10 years old, a local reporter called him "The Great One." That nickname stuck for the rest of his career. Even though Gretzky played in a high-scoring era with some of the game's greatest players, he stood out among them.

After his stellar debut season in the NHL, Gretzky only got better. He led the league in points in each of his first eight seasons in the NHL. In 1981–82, he racked up a record 92 goals and 212 points.

Gretzky led the NHL in goals in five separate seasons during his career.

Gretzky's play helped make the Oilers a title contender each season. After early playoff exits in his first three years, the Oilers reached their first Stanley Cup Final in 1983.

They faced the dominant New York Islanders, who had won three straight championships. The Oilers were no match for the powerhouse, as the Islanders swept them in four games. It was a low moment for Gretzky and his teammates. After the Game 4 loss, they walked by the New York locker room and were surprised when they didn't see the Islanders players celebrating. They were all exhausted from another long playoff run. This experience let Gretzky know the amount of work it would take to become a champion.

The motivated Oilers got back to the Stanley Cup Final in 1984. They faced the Islanders

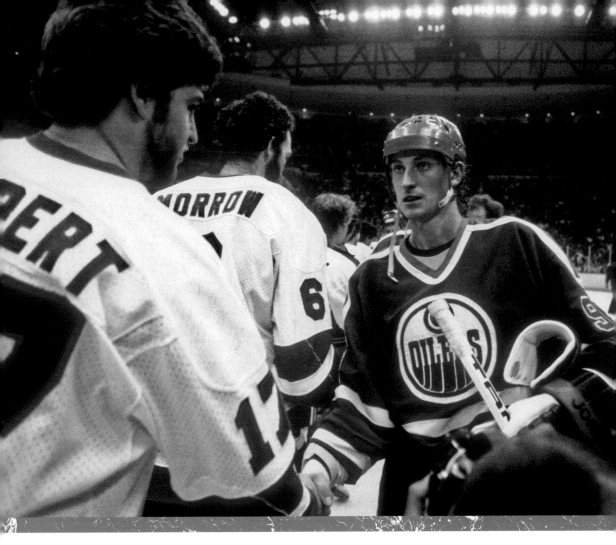

Gretzky shakes hands with New York Islanders players after the Oilers lost the 1983 Stanley Cup Final.

again. After the Oilers took a 3–1 series lead, Gretzky scored two goals in the first period of Game 5. The Oilers held on for a 5–2 victory in

front of their home fans to earn their first Stanley Cup.

After ending the Islanders' title run, the Oilers started one of their own. Gretzky tallied 47 points in 18 playoff games in 1985, lifting the Oilers to another championship. His performance also earned him the Conn Smythe Trophy, which goes to the MVP of the playoffs. Gretzky was on top of the hockey world, with much more success yet to come.

CANADA CUP

After winning multiple Stanley Cups, Wayne Gretzky won a different trophy in the summer of 1987. Gretzky played alongside 11 other future Hockey Hall of Famers on the Canadian national team in the Canada Cup. This international tournament was held across Canada and the United States. In nine games, Gretzky tallied a tournament-high 21 points. He also assisted Mario Lemieux's tournament-winning goal in the final against the Soviet Union.

Gretzky hoists the Stanley Cup in 1984.

UNTOUCHABLE RECORDS

Wayne Gretzky put up mind-blowing stats throughout his NHL career. He rewrote the league's record book almost by himself. In fact, Gretzky held 61 NHL records when he retired in 1999.

Gretzky broke scoring records with ease. Over the course of his career, he recorded more than 200 points in a season four times. No other player has done it once. Gretzky recorded his 1,050th assist in 1988, breaking Detroit Red Wings legend Gordie Howe's record. It took Gretzky nine seasons to reach that mark, which was 17 fewer seasons than it took Howe. Gretzky's high assist numbers helped him break Howe's all-time points record in 1989. He then scored his 802nd goal in 1994, once again breaking Howe's record.

Gretzky finished his career with 2,857 points. That's 936 more than any other player. His 1,963 assists accounted for most of those. In fact, if Gretzky had never scored a goal, he would still hold the all-time points record.

Gretzky poses
with Gordie Howe
after setting
the NHL scoring
record in 1989.

GRETZKY
1851

HOWE
1850

4 HOLLYWOOD STAR

Wayne Gretzky had his best individual season in 1985–86. His 215 points that season broke his own record. And his 163 assists shattered the 135 he had in the prior season. However, the Oilers failed to make it back to the Stanley Cup Final.

The playoff woes didn't last long, though. Gretzky led the Oilers to another championship in 1987, beating the Philadelphia Flyers in seven games. They made it back-to-back titles again when they swept the Boston Bruins in

Gretzky celebrates a goal during the 1987 Stanley Cup Final.

the 1988 Final. Gretzky won his second Conn Smythe Trophy that year after tallying 13 points in the Stanley Cup Final.

It seemed as if the Oilers would continue their dominance for years. Gretzky was in the prime of his career at 27. However, Oilers' owner Peter Pocklington was worried Gretzky wouldn't re-sign with Edmonton once his contract was up. Pocklington shocked the hockey world when he traded Gretzky to the Los Angeles Kings in the summer of 1988.

Gretzky could barely speak at the press conference when the trade was announced. But while he was shedding tears, fans in Los Angeles were ecstatic. Ticket sales skyrocketed for the Kings. Home games routinely sold out to

Gretzky recorded 918 points in eight seasons with Los Angeles.

Gretzky waves to the fans in New York after playing in his final NHL game.

watch the league's biggest star. Gretzky didn't disappoint. He won the Hart Trophy in his first season with the Kings. And he led the league in points in three of his eight seasons with Los Angeles.

Hockey had yet to truly take off on the West Coast in the United States. But Gretzky helped make the region a hotbed. His talent drew huge crowds every night he stepped on the ice. And Gretzky sparked hope around the league that cities in nontraditional hockey markets could host NHL teams.

Gretzky ended his career with stints on the St. Louis Blues and New York Rangers. When he retired in 1999, he had won nine Hart Trophies, earned four Stanley Cups, and led the league in scoring 11 times. The NHL also retired the Great One's No. 99 for every team, honoring the greatest player the league had ever seen.

HUMBLE OPINION

There may be only one person who doesn't think Wayne Gretzky was the greatest hockey player ever. It's Gretzky himself. He grew up idolizing Gordie Howe and claims Howe was the greatest hockey player who ever lived.

TIMELINE

1. **Brantford, Ontario (January 26, 1961)**
   Wayne Gretzky is born.

2. **Indianapolis, Indiana (October 14, 1978)**
   Gretzky plays his first professional hockey game.

3. **Edmonton, Alberta (December 30, 1981)**
   Gretzky scores his 50th goal in the 39th game of the regular season.

4. **Edmonton, Alberta (May 19, 1984)**
   Gretzky wins his first Stanley Cup.

5. **Hamilton, Ontario (September 15, 1987)**
   Gretzky lifts Canada past the Soviet Union to win the Canada Cup.

6. **Inglewood, California (October 6, 1988)**
   Gretzky scores a goal and tallies three assists in an 8-2 win in his first game with the Los Angeles Kings.

7. **Edmonton, Alberta (October 15, 1989)**
   Gretzky tallies his 1,851st point to become the NHL's all-time leading scorer.

8. **Manhattan, New York (April 18, 1999)**
   Gretzky records his 1,963rd career assist in his last NHL game while playing for the New York Rangers.

MAP

AT A GLANCE

Birth date: January 26, 1961

Birthplace: Brantford, Ontario

Position: Center

Size: 6 feet (183 cm),
185 pounds (84 kg)

Teams: Indianapolis Racers
(1978), Edmonton Oilers
(1978-88), Los Angeles Kings
(1988-96), St. Louis Blues
(1996), New York Rangers
(1996-99)

Major awards: Stanley
Cup champion (1984-85,
1987-88), Hart Trophy
(1980-87, 1989), Conn Smythe Trophy (1985, 1988), Art Ross Trophy
(1981-87, 1990-91, 1995), Hockey Hall of Fame (1999)

GLOSSARY

assists
Passes, rebounds, or deflections that result in goals.

contract
A written agreement that keeps a player with a team for a certain amount of time.

elite
The best of the best.

era
A period of time.

hat trick
When a player scores three or more goals in a single game.

points
Statistics that a player earns by scoring a goal or having an assist.

prodigy
A young person with exceptional skill.

slap shot
A shot in which a player winds up and slaps the puck with great force.

TO LEARN MORE

Books

Coleman, Ted. *Edmonton Oilers*. Mendota Heights, MN: Press Room Editions, 2023.

Hewson, Anthony K. *Hockey Records*. Lake Elmo, MN: Focus Readers, 2020.

Walker, Tracy Sue. *Wayne Gretzky: The Great One*. Minneapolis: Lerner Publications, 2023.

More Information

To learn more about Wayne Gretzky, go to **pressboxbooks.com/AllAccess**.

These links are routinely monitored and updated to provide the most current information available.

INDEX